VIENNA 1900

PEPIN®

GIFT & CREATIVE PAPERS

VOLUME

(74)

English

Vienna 1900

Vienna in 1900 saw a creative shift in art, decoration, and pattern. It was part of a fundamental movement towards a break with the traditions of the past in order to create the new traditions of the future.
Many of the new and dynamic artists and designers in turn of the century Vienna were part of the Secessionist movement, which was founded in direct competition to the conservative Vienna Academy, an institution that had grown tired, timid, and complacent.
Pattern work was an integral part of the new Secessionist dynamism in Vienna. Many of the original contemporary designs were produced by a range of young innovative individuals, such as Josef Hoffmann, Koloman Moser and Dagobert Peche.
Inspiration for this new form of pattern design came from many sources, some new and dynamic, some old and timeless. Nature was a particularly common theme, as was the abstraction of geometry. However, Japanese design also had a big impact on the new pattern work; the arts of Japan were known in Vienna through, among others, its display at International Exposition of 1873. The handcrafting, choice of natural materials and subdued decoration were qualities greatly appreciated by the Secessionists and they devoted an entire exhibition to Japanese art and design in 1903.
The new pattern work encompassed the organic as well as the geometrical, the warm swirl of nature, and the cool straight lines of the abstract. Both were to become integral in the development of modern pattern work in the twentieth century, and both have left their dynamic mark on the history of the decorative arts.

Français

Vienne 1900

Dans la Vienne de 1900, le monde de l'art et de la décoration connaît une véritable révolution créative, phénomène lié à un mouvement fondamental souhaitant rompre avec les traditions passées, afin de modeler celles de l'avenir.
De nombreux créateurs de l'époque participèrent à cette nouvelle dynamique artistique. Ce courant, dit Sécessionniste, fut créé pour concurrencer l'Académie de Vienne, institution conservatrice devenue désuète, pédante et ennuyeuse.
Le travail sur les motifs constitua une part non négligeable de ce courant innovant. Un nombre important d'œuvres contemporaines virent le jour grâce à un petit groupe de jeunes créateurs, parmi lesquels Josef Hoffmann, Koloman Moser et Dagobert Peche.
Puisant leur inspiration dans de nombreuses sources, originales et neuves, anciennes et intemporelles, la nature y tenait un rôle récurrent, à l'instar de thèmes abstraits issus de la géométrie. Le design japonais, introduit à Vienne lors l'Exposition Internationale de 1873, eut également une influence sur ces travaux. Sa production artisanale, l'utilisation de matériaux naturels et sa sobriété formaient un ensemble de qualités très appréciées des sécessionnistes. Ils consacrèrent une exposition entière au design et à l'art nippon en 1903.
Les motifs englobaient aussi bien l'organique que le mathématique, le chaud tourbillon de la nature aussi bien que les lignes droites et froides. Ces deux tendances participèrent grandement au caractère unique du motif moderne et ont laissé leur empreinte sur l'histoire des arts décoratifs.

Deutsch

Wien 1900

Um 1900 erlebte Wien in Kunst, Dekoration und Musterdesign eine kreative Veränderung. Sie ging von einer grundlegenden Bewegung aus, die mit der Tradition der Vergangenheit brach und sich aufmachte, neue Traditionen für die Zukunft zu schaffen.
Viele der neuen und progressiven Künstler und Designer im Wien der Jahrhundertwende gehörten zur Bewegung der Wiener Secession, die in direkter Konkurrenz zum müde, zaghaft und selbstgefällig gewordenen konservativen Wiener Künstlerhaus gegründet wurde.
Die dynamische Kraft der Wiener Secession ging zu einem wesentlichen Teil vom Musterdesign aus. Viele der modernen Muster wurden von jungen, innovativen Künstlern wie Josef Hoffmann, Koloman Moser und Dagobert Peche entworfen.
Sie bezogen ihre Inspiration für diese neue Art des Musterdesigns aus zahlreichen Quellen, von denen einige neu und dynamisch, andere durchaus alt und zeitlos waren. Die Natur war, ebenso wie die geometrische Abstraktion, ein besonders verbreitetes Thema. Aber auch das japanische Design hatte großen Einfluss auf die neuen Musterentwürfe. Die japanische Kunst wurde auf der Internationalen Weltausstellung von 1873 gezeigt und war unter anderem deshalb in Wien bekannt. Die Sezessionisten schätzten die handwerkliche Arbeit, die Wahl natürlicher Materialien und die dezente Dekoration ganz besonders und widmeten japanischer Kunst und japanischem Design 1903 eine ganze Ausstellung.
Die neuen Muster nahmen sowohl Organisches als auch Geometrisches auf, die warm anmutenden Spiralformen der Natur, und die kühlen, geraden Linien des Abstrakten. Beides sollte wesentlich zur Entwicklung moderner Designmuster im 20. Jahrhundert beitragen und beides hat eine dynamische Prägung in der Geschichte dekorativer Kunst hinterlassen.

Español

Viena 1900

En 1900 Viena experimentó un giro creativo en el arte, la decoración y los patrones, como parte de un movimiento principal hacia la ruptura con las tradiciones del pasado para crear las nuevas tradiciones del futuro.
Muchos de los nuevos dinámicos artistas y diseñadores de la Viena de final de siglo formaban parte del movimiento secesionista vienés, fundado en competencia directa con la conservadora Academia de Viena, una institución agotada, huraña y pagada de sí misma.
El trabajo de patrones es un elemento esencial del nuevo dinamismo de la Secesión de Viena. Muchos de sus diseños contemporáneos originales fueron elaborados por un abanico de jóvenes artistas innovadores, como Josef Hoffmann, Koloman Moser y Dagobert Peche.
Las fuentes de inspiración para esta nueva forma de diseño de patrones fueron variadas, algunas nuevas y dinámicas, otras viejas y eternas. La naturaleza junto con la abstracción geométrica fueron temáticas especialmente recurrentes. Sin embargo, el diseño japonés también tuvo una gran influencia sobre el nuevo diseño de patrones. El arte japonés se introdujo en Viena en parte gracias a su exhibición en la Exposición Universal de 1873. La artesanía, la selección de materiales naturales y la contención decorativa fueron cualidades muy apreciadas por los miembros del movimiento secesionista, quienes dedicaron una exposición exclusiva al arte y el diseño japonés en el año 1903.
El nuevo trabajo de patrones abarcó tanto lo orgánico como lo geométrico, las dulces espirales de la naturaleza y las frías líneas rectas de lo abstracto. Ambas estaban llamadas a ser parte esencial del desarrollo de los patrones modernos del siglo XX, y ambas han dejado su huella dinámica en la historia de las artes decorativas.

Cover of an edition of *Ver Sacrum* ('sacred spring'), the official magazine of the *Wiener Seccession* movement. The image is by Koloman Moser.

Copyright © 2017 Pepin van Roojen

All rights reserved. No part of this book may be reproduced or transmitted in any form or by any means without permission in writing from The Pepin Press BV.

PEPIN®

Pepin® is a trademark of Pepin Holding BV

Published by
The Pepin Press BV
P.O. Box 10349
1001 EH Amsterdam, The Netherlands
mail@pepinpress.com

www.pepinpress.com

Concept & Design
Pepin van Roojen

Introduction
John Hopper

ISBN 978 94 6009 086 8

This book is produced by The Pepin Press in Amsterdam and Singapore.